Love
Ascending

Love
Ascending

Ruth de Menezes

TRINITY COMMUNICATIONS
MANASSAS, VIRGINIA

© Trinity Communications 1987

ISBN 0-937495-18-2

Ruth de Menezes was first published as a non-Catholic poet in her youth. She converted to Catholicism in her thirties and devoted the following years to her family, during which time she did little writing. In the late 1970's she returned to her poetic craft, and soon won publication in a variety of Catholic newspapers and magazines. Soon after, she published her first book of poems, *Woman Songs*. In 1987, Mrs. de Menezes won the award for best poetry from the Catholic Press Association. In all, she has been published in over forty magazines and anthologies. One of the finest Catholic poets writing today, Mrs. de Menezes lives with her husband in Santa Monica, California.

For Catherine,
lately of Siena . . .

ACKNOWLEDGMENT

Many of the poems in this collection have been
previously published. We acknowledge with
appreciation the courtesy of the editors of
America, the New Catholic World, the St. Anthony
Messenger, Visions, Sisters Today, and Religion for
Religious who have given permission,
written or implied, for certain poems to be reprinted.

Table of Contents

PREFACE

ASYMMETRY

"The universe is built askew.
There's something in the very heart of it
That's out of plumb, and this is good
For symmetry is cursed with barrenness."
So wise men say, while poets cry, "Of course!"

How else could Cleopatra's eyes
And the squat bullfrog's staring orbs
Gaze equally on the beckoning skies?
The crumbled brick, the door hung so it will not close
Leave apertures for biologic rhapsodies—
Mutations, whims, mistakes that maybe are not quite,
And nurse a universe so crammed with wonders and delightful games
That all we children can but dance and say,
"How sweet the words that nearly, but not truly, rhyme!"
While in the curtained study wise men write
Quantum equations, pondering day and night,
The poets scurry through the rafters of the infinite roof
Searching with laughter for the nuts of truth.

7

I
Let us rejoice . . .

BE AS BROAD WINGS

Be as broad wings, my heart;
Like talons, my mind.

Hurtle screaming into the sunless depths.
Seize the struggling truth
And savage it!

APERTURES

Let us rejoice in what young Catherine knew—
That each of us is simply nothingness.
Then through the fluted docile rounds
With cosmic breath, Alpha can blow
Whatever deathless music He desires
While sweet Omega smiles, at last to hear
The tunes He dreamed eternities ago.

WRITTEN ON THE AIR

Upon the air, in sweet accord,
Their flying fingers swiftly trace
Their silent praise of You, O Lord.
How happily, with what white grace
They make a most ethereal prayer
Of symbols written upon air.

How dear their psalm must seem to You
Who love to speak in symbols, too!

MEASURELESS

Obedient to His Mother's wish,
    He stands against the wall
And Mary, measuring, laughs with joy
    To find Him grown so tall,

Forgetting as she bends to count
    Each precious inch again
That here is He Whom all of earth
    And Heaven cannot contain,

Until she meets His glance and sees
    Deep in His limpid eyes
A sweet, benignant, watchful smile—
    Old, old, and wise.

GIFTS

We cannot make, create, invent —
We who are zeroes only in a mighty sum!
Like an indulgent mother who contrives a fête
For all the cherished children she so loves,
Hiding a thousand gifts for them to hunt
In a great game of hide and seek,
God leaves His ribboned packets here and there.

The first musician found a hollow reed
Obedient to the principles of air.
Primal poets bent above
The stones that later Shakespeare wrote about
And Giotto searched and found
Perspective's laws that had been made
When this our universe was first a diagram.

These godly presents all brought joy
But be forewarned
For any gift that you accept
Brings magic with it.
You will hear
The sound of voices that you cannot prove.
You will see
Mysterious matters never to be spoken of
And you will stand forever in an unseen ring of fire
Powerless to move.

HOME

In times gone by devoutly I believed
That my particular dear home was this
Small cottage wreathed in fragrant clematis,
My happy shelter, shuttered and low-eaved.
Here was my work and joy; and I perceived
The world's wide acres with shy prejudice
And had I left my tiny benefice,
I would have been lonely; I would have grieved.

Now could I make the pampas my wide hearth,
Play in the east and labor in the west,
For since I learned He bears this little earth
Like a bright jewel hidden in His breast,
Mountain and prairie, desert and the sea—
All of the world He loves is home to me.

GLORIOUS SUM

The wise men say that while Our brave Lord died
    Upon the Cross, He suffered every pain
    The world had known or would endure again:
He cried the tears that Adam cried;
    He rode with Louis in the headsman's cart;
    Unborn Francesca's anguish tore His Heart;
He bled of wounds received in Sicily
And drowned with Shelley in an alien sea.
    The agony of every German Jew
    He also knew.

It follows then that on some splendid day
    He also must have known the glorious sum
    Of all men's joys gone by and yet to come:
Millions of children laughing at their play,
    A multitude of lovers lost in love,
    Vast works and studies, and the joy thereof.
He knew Cornelia's felicity,
The young Theresa's startled ecstacy,
    Colombo's late, emblazoned hour,
    And Mendel's pleasure in the governed flower;
Dante's beatitude and Raphael's bliss,
The tenderness of little Juliet's kiss—
    All these were His.

And as no one but God was great enough
    To bear the whole world's pain,
    Its torment and its sin,
So only Jesus could sustain
    The rapturous centuries of joy and love
    Men have delighted in.

PRAYER OF A PRIEST

On this immaculate year's initial day
Before Thy holy altar, Lord, I pray

The sonorous and lovely Latin Mass;
And when Thy people tremulously pass

Along the aisles and to the gleaming rail
And I have tasted once again Thy Grail,

I bow my head in prayer: Lord, through this year
Help me to shepherd well Thy white flock here.

Bless those who kneel, unknowing and unknown,
Whose days to come are plain to Thee alone.

Here are the unbetrothed, whose nuptials I
Shall before winter bless and sanctify.

Here are the mothers, bright with sons and daughters
Whom one day I shall wash with living waters.

Here are the aged, and some young and merry,
Whom I shall in a brief time shrive and bury.

Lord, in Thy great compassion let them see
That lover, child and death—they all are Thee!

PSALM

I brought a single flower to Your tabernacle, Lord,
And You presented me with mountains.
Before Your altar I offered you the cricket song of my adoration,
And the heavens were filled with the chanting of ten thousand angels.
I placed the candle flame of my love on Your table,
And You thrust the burning sun into my arms.

Who am I that You should overwhelm me with blessings?
For my spirit has the strength of a match stick.
My spirit has the depth of a raindrop
And the majesty of a grain of sand.

Lord, in times past my neck was of stone,
My knees were without joints; my heart was filled with pride.
But now I shall be like a cloud going before a great wind.

Blow me wherever You will, O Lord, and I shall go rejoicing.
Send me over the prairies and the hills;
Dispatch me to the deserts; enjoin me to traverse the seas.
Your will is mine. Your will is my perpetual delight.
Or in Your wisdom utterly disperse me
And with my ultimate breath I will cry out,
"So shall it be. Praised be the Name of the Lord!"

ONE BODY

Devour and live.
Shakespeare sustains you
And my lyrics, too,
Turn now and sink
Through depths on depths
Of your forever mind.
A simple cell, I hurry,
Jostling, to repair your wound.
"To each his own"
But who is each when each is all?
It's plain as bones upon a beach!
He said, "Take me and eat"
And that's not rhetoric!
Oh take, take, take!
This is the mystery,
And mystery's the answer!

ANNUNCIATIONS

A time for prayer,
Before the strident sun
Clangs like a gong
Upon the brown edge of the hills.

There never was a stillness such as this
Where all of waiting nature was struck dumb.
No bird, no seeking cicada, no smallest breeze
Presumed to speak.

In utter quietude, with lowered eyes
And acquiescent hands
Folded in prayer,
The perfect maiden waited in the dawn.

The new day in its delicate hues
Of palest azure and amethystine pearl
Trembled to find this lady at her prayers
Who seemed herself created out of light.

Then in the stillness came a gentle sound—
The furling of great wings.
The universe leaned close to hear the angel's words,
And when she understood at last and said, "I will,"
The immemorial star began to move
Toward Bethlehem.

This was the unrepeated miracle we know
Performed in purest silence and in purest light,
But since that hour, time after time,
In stinking alleys and tawdry, sweated rooms,
On jangling trains, in offices and laundromats,
In bars and discos, the sound of furling wings is heard.
A leaning angel whispers, "Will you take this Child
And cherish Him, and give Him to the world?"
And for a lightning space the earth is still
While painted lips, surprised and stammering, reply,
"I will."

VOCATION

She said she wished to be a shrub
And sit in silence, lost, obscure
In some dim woods where no one ever comes
And she could muse and watch the quiet winds go by.

But He who long ago observed a brambled bush
Looked at her once among the ferns.
He looked but once; the winds became a storm
And now she burns, she burns!

ZENITH

Now at its zenith burns my life's own sun;
The circle of my loving is complete,
And I go gowned in love from head to feet,
My pride struck down, my wilfulness undone.
Seek out no greater love, for there is none.
Love lights my eyes, impels my heart to beat;
I read my love, and it is love I eat;
With love each day is ended and begun.

Would I were Joshua so that I might
Command my sun to pause at my sweet noon
And let me love at leisure, who so soon
Will know the growing dusk and then the night.
Love well, my heart, and in far-distant skies
I may in some great dawn see God arise!

II
The way it really was . . .

NEWS

There is more news than that of terror, greed and war
But it is hidden like a wintering seed.
Many a Bethlehem, unnoted, dreams
Without angelic music or a star
Or rustic shepherds hurrying forth.

Lord, in your mercy make my ears and eyes
Alert to common goodness everywhere
And in the chaos of these tearful days
Hold my heart steady to your north!

SHOPPING MALL

One day while waiting in a shopping mall
With light and busy-ness and people all about
I took my book and read.
My body heard the bells of noon begin.
By then my thoughts were in a distant galaxy;
When they returned, the chimes struck one.
Where had time gone?
The answer came to me: time does not go,
For time is truly not.

And then I thought someday I might sit here
Lost in old words that take me far away
Until perhaps at last I see the pages have gone gold
And my two hands that hold the book—*my* hands?—are old!

Then I might raise my body's eyes to see
Nothing but rubble in a smokey square,
The tall, proud buildings all dispersed,
Trees, flowers, people everywhere
Vanished without a sound,
And in the silence final and profound
Where Robinson's and May's once stood,
One sad-eyed rabbit, quivering with pain and cold
Drenched in his own blood.

The clocks of earth were ticking when the skies were riven
But the holocaust had roots, I think, in timeless Hell
And soot drifts now along the marble floors of Heaven
Where no chime ever sounds, or measured bell . . .

INTERIORS

My dear, you should see her house!
It's gorgeous, simply gorgeous!
Done by the best in Beverly Hills, of course:
Parquet floors, Oriental rugs,
Great windows draped in silk,
And furniture that speaks of other times
When craftsmen loved their work.
Those classic lines, the sheen,
The richness of those antique woods!
And naturally, Picassos on the walls.

Please understand,
For I believe in beauty such as this,
And that as wise men say,
It mirrors beauty that's in Heaven.

But oh, my dear, you should look into her mind!
Empty, empty, empty!
And a dank wind blowing through,
Stirring the rubbish in the corners!

YOUNG MAN IN A FAST CAR

Like some wild birdling stolen from his nest
That somehow still remembers liberty
And now forever in a fluttering rage
Shrieks and beats against his cage's cold gray bars,
So he rides out the freeway's rapids with fine scorn.
Something more majestic than his mind
Informs his racing blood that he is really air
And that he can, or should, transcend each sign's demands,
Passing unscathed around—or even through—each careful car.
For him, danger inevitably is never there.
Churchless, his look and actions still declare
He thinks he truly is as swift as thought
And through his heritage, untouched by space and time.

The bright words blazoned on his bumptious bumper say
"I brake for naked women" but his silent cry
Is simply, "I am life and universal love. *Make way!*"

SLOW

I am not finished with the splendors of this earth
Nor have I solved its many mysteries.

How busy and intrigued you are
(And rightly so) with bangs and holes
And countless stars beyond your sight!

Run then with calculus about the universe
While I stand mesmerized beside our sea
Staring at light upon a tossing wave,
Or lost in wonder at a weed.

Arrange for tourist travel to our satellite;
Move in your myriads into other worlds,
But keep in mind that I am slow and never soon.
Often I look at space and hope to see
A happy cow that leaps above the moon.

THE LADY

They say
This lady is as lovely as an April day
And she is good as saints are good.

I met this woman once.
We stood upon a morning lawn
Speaking perhaps a hundred casual words,
But then she chanced to bow her head and saw
A snail sleepwalking on the grass.
With laser speed she raised a dainty boot,
Thrust downward once and smiled to see
The snail a sticky nothing on the ground.

This lady's loveliness of face and mind
Are attributes I never can recall
But her swift resolution of the snail is with me still—
And that is all.

THE OLD MAN

He reads throughout the night
And all day long, he dreams.
The ancient horsemen thunder over head
Without his noting.
Terror, wars, disease and death
Pass like trivial clouds
Across his sky.
Impassive as a sundial,
He reflects only the light.

THE MIRROR

If only this gold bordered glass would show
The boy who looked in it so long ago,
And from its crystal depths there would arise
Once more his face. Oh, if his smiling eyes
Gazed into mine again, how quickly I would bend
To press a kiss upon his pale cool cheek
And tell him of my love!
Alas, his image does not reappear;
The glass is bleak with emptiness.
No hint of him, however delicate, is here.
A mirror always shows not more, but less . . .

POSSESSION

All I have loved is mine forevermore.
　　Last winter's rapturous and perfect rose
Blooms now as sweetly as she did before,

　　Nor is there any earthly wind that blows
That has the power to set one petal free.
　　The hours die, but beauty never does,

And my far mountains and the far-off sea,
　　Flowers and faces and music I have known—
A thousand things that have enchanted me

　　Enchant me yet, and never will be gone;
　　Because I loved them, now they are my own.

Along these streets, I tread a mountain trail;
　　I watch the surf upon a distant shore;
Within my ears sound notes that never fail,

　　And tender voices I shall hear no more;
While like some blossomy and hidden glen,
　　My heart wears all the flowers the year once wore.

And you, the lost one, gentlest of men,
　　Lover of poesy and sarabands,
Speak with me still, though now a citizen

　　Of wild and inaccessible dark lands.
I hear your words, and while I dare not stir,
　　You innocently lean to kiss my hands.

The clocks are silent, and the walls a blur;
The rose blooms on, and you are as you were.

THE TRAVELER

She murmurs in her faint old voice
That she has yet to see the world, and sighs,
And though I tell her of the greatly traveled Kant
Who never knew a hill beyond his home,
She does not see the distance she has come.

She once enjoyed the land of living love
And then crossed over to a region rich with pain,
Making her patient way, in time,
To love again.

She has explored the shadowed vales of grief
And flown her banner from an Everest of joy.
Up, down and all about, her life has taken her.
She seems to me a truly valiant traveler.

Now soon upon a white sailed ship she will embark
On joyous waters for an unmapped land
Where all our storied journeys, brief or long,
Must ultimately end.

IN PRAISE OF HELEN

This is the way it really was
Though no one knows but I, great Priam's son.

Menelaus, proud and cold, had always passed me by
But Aphrodite found a place for me within his house
And soon my eyes and Helen's met.

I paid my homage to her with great joy
And fed her heart with songs and fantasies.
She looked and listened, and I watched her turn
The gossamer of her thoughts to me
As flowers bend their petals toward the light.
Like some young careless boy upon a beach
Who builds a tower of pebbles and adds one more, one more
And holds his breath for fear the tower will fall,
So I would vow to her my lasting love
And weave a hundred lies and hold my breath
Lest she draw back and cry a halt. She never did.
By all the gods, she heard me out!

One immemorial night, we stole away
Before the moon crept up, and in my tent
We leapt together like two fiery stars.
I knew at last the softness of her breasts,
The breathless kisses and the clasping thighs
And thought of Menelaus.

If I had known then of the thousand ships
And all the years to come of war and death,
I would have wooed this lovely woman still.
She was my victory, my proof I towered over Menelaus
Who always saw me with contempt.

When finally she slept within my arms
And all my joy and pride, like a great fire,
Dwindled and sank,
Long did I look upon her in the moonlit night
And revelled in the gifts that Helen bore:
The gift of perfect beauty that the gods had given;
The jewels—from Menelaus—entwined and sparkling in her hair;
The pearls—from Menelaus—that graced her throat;
And underneath the breasts that softly rose and fell,
Her golden girdle, all be-gemmed—from Menelaus—
Still snug around her willing waist.

I heard a cock crow thrice and raised my eyes.
The moon had gone. I felt the chill of morn
And as I drew the furs about us both,
I knew her crowning gift: snug in her rosy loins
The loathsome viper of my scorn.

A BOMB CALLED "LITTLE BOY"

A dazzling kind of beauty is my pride
And I, the angel Lucifer, seem strong and sure
But in my seething center burns
A writhing snake of fire
That bites and burns with my imperial desire
And my proud throat is choked with maggot-ridden venom—
Such is my rage against the One who made me.

I have sworn to overcome Him.
Oh, what nuclear laughter will ring out
When my own will, not His, controls the universe!

I have done well, so far.
I often only smile and wink
To have His creatures run with laughter to my knee.
They learn my devious lessons eagerly and well.
Only when that fair Child was born beneath a star
Was I befuddled for a century or two.
He soon began to talk of love and Him whose name I cannot speak
And He had followers. Where is He now?

This is my truth: I am available
And they can find me anywhere.
I have so much to offer—
Wealth, position, power, joy and praise.
In fact, my stock soars day by day
For now the forces of the universe
Stir and tremble in their faltering hands.
Knowing them as I do, I also know
How like brainless sheep they are.
Even the bees are wiser and more organized.
Through men I will defeat the planning of my Enemy
Who fathered, it is said, a Son.

Faugh! He is *not* the only one!
My secret agony begins to ease
And laughter bubbles in my fetid throat.
Let it be written, it shall come to pass
That in the manger of Los Alamos
An iron child will soon be born
And they shall call him "Little Boy."
He will be haloed with horror beyond words,
Fated to fly with hellish gifts above Hiroshima.
So from small beginnings will come total death.
Now I can crush His earth as though it were a baby's toy
And He who loves all men can only weep. . . .
For I, great Lucifer, have fed His sheep.

III
By God's courtesy . . .

GRAMMAR

The loops and marks of grammar
    Seem often here and there—
The comma of the infant moon,
    The full stop of a stair;
A hyphenating snail at dawn
    Recording his little where

And then, of course, and more than this,
    Love's parenthesis.

FAIRY FIDDLER

In the grasses, in the dark
While sleep the throstle and the lark,
Hear the tiny fiddler fiddling
With a most exquisite diddling!
Who makes music sweet as this,
Delicate as moonlight is—
Rising miniature and sweet
From the flowers at my feet?

What fair fiddler weaves for me
A lullaby so wee?

Is it
Possibly
A cricket?

SIAMESE CAT

The Maker has given me quite a fine world:
Flowers and shrubs to sniff and sleep under,
Trees to climb, birds to chase,
Fences to walk upon,
And a two-legged creature always ready
    to assist with any problems.

Most of all, I love the darkness.
When the sun sets and a new night begins,
I stretch myself and go forth into the shadows
Where I delight in moving delicately,
In perfect silence,
Deliberating on all things different or new,
Meeting old friends,
Enjoying the midnight breezes and the multitudinous fragrances.

I understand the universe presented to me
But in the morning after milk,
On folded paws, with half-closed eyes,
I wonder why the Maker made two-legged creatures
Who shout and thunder through the dazzling day . . .
Doubtless He had His reasons.

Meanwhile, let us thank Him for His blessings—
For the night that always comes again,
For the stillness, the solitude, the immemorial dark.

I prowl; therefore I am.

STRAY CAT

The gray cat mewed and milk appeared
In a blue bowl on the floor
Thrust quickly by a nameless hand
Through a slightly opened, guarded door.

She drank and praised Him with a purr
And now in trust that is complete,
She sleeps luxuriantly on the stony step
Made for the tenants' hurrying feet.

We all tiptoe around this somnolent heap of fur
Moving adroitly with exquisite care,
Seeing so clearly the faith she has in Him
As He, no doubt, has total faith in her.

THE DEATH OF A CAT

I loved him,
Proud and furry friend.
Now he is gone,
But he has left me an enduring legacy—
A bluebird's feather on the summery lawn.

PATROL

Now moon and earth dance out their pas de deux
And in the ballet of the spheres the world
Spins tilting toward the outer reaches of the sky,
Turning its back upon the fecund sun.
The monstrous megalopolis sleeps.
There are no sheep to guard, no tigers on the street.
The pavements are at peace, but still
There comes from far away the distant bark
Of one unsleeping dog, lifting his voice
Against some danger in the winter night.

It must have been millennia ago
That members of some family sheltering in a cave
Would likewise stir and lift their heads to hear
A wolfish friend patrolling far below;

And many centuries from now
When seas and nations have been swept away
The last, the ultimate man will hear
As he sinks down midst ashes by an empty stream
Not thunder in the dark, or angels' songs,
But faintly on the winds of night
The far off barking of a dog.

THE ANT

How desperately he searches for the way,
Lost in a world he cannot see.
Quickly he runs now here, now there
Along your resting leg up to your knee
And does not know he scouts
Thereafter on your palm that does not close.
If you should speak to him in purest Antnamese
And whisper that you wish him well,
Then tell him your particular name,
Your past and present and that you hold
The future in your hand,
Do you believe that he would understand?

Or as you gently slip him back among his peers,
Will he exult, still unaware: "Once I was lost
But now am found. How lucky can I be!"

THROUGH AN OPEN WINDOW

Oh pity not the passionate pale moths
Beating their wings upon the golden candle flame!
Oh pity not the moths!

What sweeter death could you devise for them?
Would you prefer them drowned by busy rains?
Broken by heedless winds? devoured by birds?

No . . . Let the candle be. Not without wisdom
Do these exquisite frail creatures seek the flame.
Here in a swift communion with perfect beauty
They take a lovely leave of the imperfect night.
I think that many a mortal would be glad
To come upon a death as quick and bright!

Oh pity not the moths!

BUTTERFLY

See this lovely resurrection,
    Glorious and miniature!
Now the worm, on brief reflection,
    Assumes his bright investiture.

Lightly on alien, gold wings
    He goes a new, exotic way
And with exquisite flutterings
    Dances into the summer day.

With what a dainty skill he flits
    Along the strange paths of the air
And delicately skims and skits
    Among the azure breezes there.

Were you amazed at this translation
    From dark cocoon to shining skies?
Fancy the butterfly's elation—
    His tiny and intense surprise!

ON VIEWING A DOCUMENTARY

The camera moves its lens, and now we see
Some twenty feet above the chanting choir
And nearer Heaven, that some presumptious spider has surveyed
The isolated space, marked out the points of wings and crowns
And in between
Deftly made visible his gifts of filigree.
With swirl after filmy swirl
From Michael's lance to cherub to God's girl
He has proclaimed his reverence in these holy halls.

Perhaps one day this cherished church will sleep
Like Beauty, hidden in the silent wood
With all its wonders gently wrapped and swathed
Until at last the hurrying Prince appears to take
His waiting bride, and with shouts and music and great words
The webs are torn away and all awake!

THRENODY

Silent, mysterious, aloof,
And delicately dressed in gold,
You dwelt within a crystal room
With gleaming water for your roof
And for your furniture, a stone;
And all who passed you might behold
How quiet was your way of life,
As tranquil, thoughtful, and alone
You slumbered, waved your fins, and ate,
Untouched by passion, greed, or strife.
Granting no favors, asking none,
You were content to meditate
And softly swim from sun to sun.

But yesterday a sudden change
Swept through your world; a passing boy
Who pitied you your Spartan role
Placed a great rose within your bowl,
And laughing, lightly wished you joy.
First, startled by the lovely bloom,
You fled and hid behind the stone;
Then, more assured, you warily
Approached your guest, admired her strange
Bright velvet fins, her long green tail,
Until at last, won over, grown
More used to beauty, you swam up
And reveled in her sweet perfume.

Alas! At dawn we found you pale
And pitifully still with death;
The flower that brought you happiness
Had robbed you of your golden breath . . .
And now I wonder, little fish,
As you were dying, did you wish
That life for you had always been
A bowl, some water and a stone?—
That you had never, never known
The glory of a scarlet fin?

Or were you rapt with wonder and delight,
And did you gladly die, as one who goes
Deeming death a trivial forfeit for a night
Of intimacy with a rose?

A CERTAIN BIRD

There is a bird here that thinks that darkness
    is a splendid time
For studying music. Each night he wakes
To practise rapturously the phrases he was born to sing
And make the listening midnight ring.

Apparently he knows through some report
That art is long and life is short.

I can imagine all his friends squeezing their angry
    eyes tight
And pushing their little heads deeper
    under their wings,
While he tries again and again for pear shaped tones
And sings and sings and sings . . .
And in the dark houses people punch their pillows
    with a sigh
Hearing the proud, pure notes flung high.

But what can you do at twelve with a bird
    in a tall tree
Who thinks that day's not long enough for such as he?

EMINENCE

Tossing their heads, the birds are well aware
They have a wider view than we
And often wings will take one farther than a thought.

But sometimes I grow weary as they sit
Dressing their shining feathers for the joy of it,
Pluming themselves as if they wished to say,
"Observe, oh wingless men, what God has wrought!"

I wonder as their feathers flash and gleam,
How they can fly, so full of self-esteem!

THE BOWER BIRD

He goes in gray and has no song to sing
    And so to please the sweet bird of his choice
He builds a bower of flowers and pretty stones
    Which he arranges with devoted care.

He cannot guess
    She does not give a warble for his dress
Or that the hoarseness of his singular voice
    Sounds rapturously in her ear.
Oh bower bird, she only wants you near!

THE SWIFTS

Suddenly out of the trees a cloud of birds
    Springs into the lonely sky,
Soaring and circling together with twinkling wings.
    In silence I watch them fly.

I see them wheeling with strange intentness,
    Moving in mystical circles through the light,
And I hear the delicate whispering of their wing beats,
    Hushed and remote in the ecstacy of flight.

Over and over they soar through the sky and turn
    And soar again—I wish I knew
Whom in the luminous air of evening
    They rapturously pursue.

QUESTION

He lifts his massive head to look about
With piercing amber eyes, then bends again,
Untouched by guile, to taste the blood upon his gilded claws.
He and all his fellows, armored and furred,
Fashioned of feathers or scales or rainbowed gauze
Are unrestricted by the ancient laws
That speak to us of rectitude long lost.

We must become as children, it is said,
To enter Heaven,
But nature's darlings need not change.
They seem beyond beatitudes
And with a terrible majesty
Live all their lives in perfect innocence.

Is it then possible that when they gaze
With enigmatic, luminous eyes
Into the shadows that crowd about us all,
They see in silence inexpressible mysteries
No human being ever sees?

TOO BY TOO

The lowing cow whose calf has been removed
Mourns at her loss and cannot see
Why she must bear the bitterness of grief—
  Like you—like me!

The bower bird, so desperate to woo
And win his lady love,
Because he cannot sing a song, makes do
With other tributes, but is troubled, too,
Because he well might fail—
  Like me—like you!

An isolated ant, frantic without friends
Since he has lost his freeway map, panics and sends
Signals of dire distress, hurtling here and there,
Hunting the proper exit in despair.
Unfortunate ant who does not have a clue—
  Like me—like you!

A novice butterfly lifts off into the air
But wonders how the landing field will be
And whether there are hawks to fear—
  Like you—like me!

The whale that cleaves the waters of the deep
Pauses from time to time to leap
Out of the ocean that is his,
Rejoicing in his marvelous expertise
And all he does that he was shaped to do—
  Like me—like you!

And cats and dogs and horses and all sorts—
The sloth that sits, the zebra that cavorts,
The eagle soaring in the infinite blue,
Know well that life is good, a glorious gift—
    And you and I, we know it, too.

The tired gray elephant, so old and wise
Looks one last time at those unfathomable skies
And slowly lets his weary magnitude
Sink to the kindly earth. His breath
Comes slower, fainter, then no more. Death
Will now encompass him who can no longer be.

    Like you. . . . Like me. . . .

LOVE ASCENDING

Heaven is not our due
And never was,
But by God's courtesy
We slip into that joy
By clinging to the coat tails of our Christ.
Sky-wide and radiant, they trail
Behind Incarnate Love ascending.

Trembling, we hold fast, and look!
In humble mimicry
The little creatures that we loved on earth—
Birds, dogs and cats and all—
Fasten themselves to our long garments, too,
And rise with us, dear God, to life with You!

IV
Tomorrow you will be more . . .

ANGLE

The countries coexist.
Frictional force
Balances perfectly
With gravity's awesome pull.
How long can this persist?
Where lies security?
Who knows?

Others may run and search,
But as for me,
I use the only army that I have.
"Love, let me lean my head
Against your heart.
You are my angle of repose."

MARRIAGE

In varied ways both fabulous and sweet
Life fosters many loves and joyfully
Marries the blossom to the honeybee
And weds the rich earth to the golden wheat.
The monk who kneels in his austere retreat
Is husband to his prayer; sagacity
Is subject to the sage; in ecstacy
The lover makes the breathless bride complete.

These are the fortunate and the enraptured,
But sighing, each could tell you if he would
That the still, secret heart of womanhood,
Of thought, of flower, remains uncaptured.
No love, however much desired and dear,
Can find its perfect consummation here.

LOVE

Many a lover to her love has said
In the sweet darkness of their honeymoon,
"Embrace me once again, beloved, for soon—
So swiftly pass the years—we shall be dead,
Translated to that land where none may wed
And where however we may importune,
Kisses are contraband, and a sad rune
Divides these two whom once love comforted."

Such grief must make the angels smile, for she
Who enters Heaven will soon discover
The terrible raptures of one Lover
And love exalted to Infinity;
While earthly love, star-constant and star-bright,
Is lost as is a star in morning light.

THE TWO BLESSINGS

Brothers and sisters, what blessings have been given us
For in our multitudes we have been born
Into an azure world in varied lands
With names like poems and we equally share
In the glory of five exquisite senses
As our radiant sphere
Twirls gently in an endless sky.

Dear friends, unknown and known,
For a little time we struggle,
Wonder and rejoice,
Then as the adamant seasons pass
And finally our splendid bodies tire and droop
We share impartially that second blessing,
Beautiful and strange—
We die. . . .

Like boys and girls with studies still undone
And many games yet waiting to be played
With drowsy eyes we sink into the cradling earth.
Let no cries of grief be heard, but only mirth!
Rejoice that now we know a sleep as free
From fear and pain as little children know,
And when the tranquil dawn returns
We all shall breakfast in eternity.

COME DOWN!

Loved and lovely though you be,
Lady dear, come down to me!
I'll grow violets from your eyes
And all my roses, white and red,
Will be a comfort for your bed
Where my warm dust will gently prove
To be your fondest, final love
With intermingling so complete
You will be lost, and find it sweet.

All that earthly eyes can see
Of you, dear one, was made from me.
I claim you now. Bend to my breast.
Sigh one more sigh. . . . and rest.

GAMES

I'm ugly now
But I'll be uglier when I'm a corpse
And quieter.
Then all my wit—or so you call it—
Will be fled
And all my laughter stilled.
I've laughed a lot—
We women are so helpless and so wrought upon
By every season's passing!
And then, like time, I have a gift for jokes
And play at subtle games with those I love.
Often I've removed myself to hide.
Now once again you'll see me gone
Although my body lies before you cold and still.
I hope you hear a whisper on the wind—
"Aha! Just try to find me *now*!"

TIME

O Time, you are a ruthless sovereign!
Up to this moment you have sent to me
Gifts of great richness and diversity,
But I perceive such lavishness will wane
And like all citizens of your domain,
I must submit to your gray alchemy,
Losing youth's color and sweet symmetry
And the bright gaiety the green sustain.

Much can you do with your persistent years
But I am not impressed; the spirit knows
That you who pity neither girl nor rose
Rule us but briefly. Give me age and tears!
I shall outwit you at the last and rise
With light laughter into the timeless skies.

DEATH

Breathless with wonder, transfixed with surprise,
I caught a glimpse of Death one Christmas Eve,
And my rapt spirit trembled to perceive
That here in this impalpable bright guise
Was perfect joy; the tongue cannot apprise
Such sweet delight, nor mortal heart conceive
His lightninged loveliness, but I believe
That all the stars of heaven were in his eyes.

So when my time for leaving life draws near,
When lover, friend and singing are no more,
Like some imprisoned lady sick to hear
The thunder of her rescuer at the door,
I shall wait Death, my cloak and gloves put on,
Watching the road, impatient to be gone.

VIGIL

At midnight there were four beneath this roof.
The doors were locked,
The windows closed against the dark.

At last the ancient clock
Spoke of the imminence of day
And lo, we now were three!

Without a word, without the opening of a door
Someone had slipped away . . .

DEAD

There was no long parade,
No muffled drums,
No horse with swinging boots reversed,
But all that day the birds were mute
While in the deepening night
The very tides were stilled
And one by one,
The stars went out.

WHERE?

Oh dear and timeless love,
    Where have you gone?—
You who were earth and light to me,
    My up, my down.

Oh warmth of my very blood,
    Breath of my quickened breath,
Rich fullness of my lack,
    Where have you gone? Oh where?
No answer stirs the air.

I'll write you then in care of death.
    Write back!

SOMETHING STRANGE

Don't ask me why or how.
Beneath the buttressed brow
My eyes look down
As when one walks beneath the blazing sun.
Don't ask me where or when.
All I know
Is something strange took place.
Life is different now
And my own skies
Are filled with brilliant, overwhelming light
So piercing and so bright
I cannot lift my eyes.
I shield my face and trembling, do not dare
To look on truth I cannot bear.

SPACE WALK

I float far off like a tiny, undiscovered star.
The linkage to the ship is broken.
A thousand years from now
A little sparkle in the mighty void
Will mark the metal of my suit
As I wheel slowly through indifferent skies,
Nameless and alone in space.
Not even a curious eagle can rise so far
To peck at glass and see my cold white face
Frozen forever in a smile
As I regard the empty everywhere
And find it not more empty than the here.

WEATHER

How hidden is the weather of the soul!
Here once a sun that only I could know
Shone in its delicate loveliness
And with my impassive face and private pulse
No one could guess my perfect happiness.

Today my secret thunder claps so loud
I wonder my companions cannot hear.
With a sibilant bolt the ruthless lightning strikes
And smoking, scores the tall tree of my mind.
All groans within and shakes with agony
As I walk calmly down the busy street
Pausing serenely at the crowded corner's sign.
None notes my smooth and careful face
While I await a greener light, an open space.

COLORS

All this was long ago.
We came one day from Berkeley's blossoming hills
To spend an hour in North Beach. I recall
We walked beneath soft skies of gray
Down windswept asphalt tilted toward the sea.
Salt steeped houses lined the empty street.
He held my hand in his and I
Went proudly like a queen, dressed in a gown
Decked out with painted blossoms of every hue—
Gold, pink and amethyst and blue—
And there were silken flowers crowning my fair hair.
Oh, I was tall with joy and love when suddenly
I saw a curtain move
And glimpsed behind the graying lace
A bent old woman's ancient face
Gray with her years,
Watching our bright parade
With piercing enigmatic eyes;
And then I knew that bit by bit,
My colors, too, would fade away
And one day I would likewise stand
Alone behind old lace gone gray,
Looking upon the young and happy going by,
And thorns, not flowers, would grace my brow.

As now.

FIRST

His hand
Is stretched to bless a planet or a rose.
Still as galactic winds not yet unbound,
He stands as tall as stars
And hears my wild heart say,
"Forgive me, but above all else
I faint, I die to look upon my love again.
Your heaven cannot be heaven for me
Until I see my dear—so loving, kind and wise.
I confess it—he is first.
A cosmic longing pierces me
And all my being inescapably
Is drawn toward him who is not here.
Forgive me, Lord," and He replies,
"Child, him whom you love, him you will see . . .
And Me." And there is laughter in His eyes.

IF

If I had only known
Death, frightened, would have fallen back
At my uplifted arms,
My furious eyes!
I would have breathed my breath
Into your fainting lungs.
I would have lain the length of me
Along your faltering body
And your smoldering blood
Would have caught fire from mine.
You would still be here
If I had only known.

But you were all alone.

LOST

O what a bonnie kingdom I once ruled
Sparkling with sunny streams and flowering fields
Where all the thousands that I met
Threw me their kisses, bowed and cheered me on . . .
How well they knew the power of my crown!
Then there were songs and dancing all day long
And fires and music in the friendly night.

Alas, my jewels have vanished and my crown is gone.
Now I go tottering through the cheerless streets,
Frail, invisible, alone.
Even a headsman would be company
And I would gladly make a cart my throne.

LOST AND GONE

Life for us was a single starry night
With birds and flowers and a moon that did not move,
And we had nothing to endure or seek or prove
As we waltzed laughing in a room all gold and white.
How beautiful the girls and fleet
While the tall boys danced them here and there
With all the silken dresses fluttering
Above the happy, flashing feet
And proud musicians played and smiled.

Sometimes we paused to chat
Or gathered at the laden board
Where the great bowls of roses seemed to guard
The delicate food, patisserie too beautiful to eat
And the pale wine the servants poured.

The rapturous hours came and went and still we danced
While the wide hems of the pastel skirts
Frothed and dipped in time with every beat
And glance met glance and lips made promises to keep.
O happy night that passed so beautifully!

Then as I and my true love swirled around the room
I saw the yawning servants rigid at the door
And shortly after, they were seen no more.
I noted then the crowd was growing sparse.
Minute by minute, to fainter music in a dimming light
Our loved and loving friends in ones and two's
Drifted away without a word.

At last the music ceased and in the lull
I heard a petal fall.
My glance fell on a dying rose;
Then when I turned to waltz again
I found my partner gone
And as I stood forlorn, alone,
The music makers took their lutes and viols
And tiptoed down the mazy halls.
The room was empty now; the dance was done
And only I, bereft, was left.

With hesitant step, I made my way
To stand before a mirror edged with gold.
"How strange," I thought, "of all the happy throng
I am the only one who lasted out the night.
Vanished are my darlings. I alone remain."

"Not true," the mirror whispered. "Look again.
Is this reflection really yours?
Yes, every one of those you loved is lost and gone.
To the roster of their names, add now your own."

LAST VOYAGE

Here lies the happy ship that trembles to depart,
Festive with flowers and ribbons linking it to shore
And those who cry farewell to her who comes no more.

One by one her lovers and her friends
Let slip the many colored silken strands
That gently break and fall among the waves
Until at last one only links the eager ship
To him who stands apart upon the pier
While the dark tides begin to froth and flow.

The great ship trembles but the trembling ribbon holds.
In God's name, let it go!

GUEST OF THE UNIVERSE

I wish to thank you for your hospitality.
It was so kind of you to let me come
And every minute was a joy to me.
Yes, I heard the noises in the streets
But as you are aware, no neighborhood
Is what it used to be!
However, you have indeed a lovely view—
All those stars and suns and moons!—
And in your house, the music was sublime.
The mysteries were lots of fun
Though hard to solve,
And I enjoyed the party's theme—*Love*,
You said it was.
That will endure forever. You can use it next time around!

Look! I am the very last of all your guests
But then, you gave me chores to do! Remember?
Now they are done and I must say good-bye and go.
The night is darkening and I'm not quite certain of the way.

You'll walk with me and see me to my door?
How kind! With you beside me, Sir,
There will be light enough and more!

A WEDDING HAS BEEN ARRANGED

Let me go lightly as a song,
    A widow once, but twice a bride,
My wedding gown a winding sheet
    Decked with a thousand pearls—
The shimmering tears I would not shed
    Because you are not truly dead.

Along a smooth and beckoning path
    Bordered with flowers, I shall glide
With caroling birds for company
    As joy and wonder lead me on
To where you watch and wait for me.

A friend and angel whom I know
    Will draw the luminous veil aside
And breathless, smiling, I shall go
    Out of the shadows, out of the pain
To embrace at last the light that is you
    And lie in the arms of love again.

PLANES

We love the horizontal plane.
The eyes can rest with joy
On the long ocean's lengthy line,
The prairie's latitude
Or the rich mesa of an open book.
We look with level looks
Deep into each other's eyes and look again.
The horizontal gives its glory to our days.

But even the widest sea
Will in some far-off century dissipate,
And books and golden plains alike
Will turn to dust and partner with the air.
Even the most beloved, breast to breast,
Must sometimes break and go.
The horizontal cannot reassure.

Only the vertical
Soaring forever beyond the evanescent stars
Endures.

POISED

As in the womb the pulsing embryo
Grows hour by hour in strength and aptitudes,
Sporting the needed spine, the precious brain,
The muscles and electric nerves,
And finally complete in every part,
Shifts in its warm and watery home and is poised
For entrance to a waiting world,
So in that very world, we weep at first
And then, surprised, rejoice,
And in the passing, rigorous years
Are pushed and prodded,
Led, persuaded, chiselled, honed,
Furbished and refurbished,
Whipped and crowned, until at last
We point toward that for which there are no words—
The world of then and now and always will.

THE UNIVERSE EXPANDS FOREVER

Consider the cosmos of your body,
The constellations of your mind!

As a woman carries her child,
I cradled you deep in My thought
    from the remote beginning.
At last you sprang like a star
    from the dark womb of your appointed mother.

Hour by hour you grow.
Your light increases like that of a rising sun.
You are not today what you were yesterday,
And tomorrow you will be more.
You constantly become.

I have shot the fiery arrow that you are
And with terrible intensity you pursue Me
Who can never be attained.
Through infinity you rush toward Me,
The half glimpsed but never overtaken.

O arrow that longs to pierce My heart
    with love and understanding
In your longing is My joy!

Come to Me, most marvelous of My marvels,
Growing ever greater as you come.

I, the unknowable Mystery,
Bless you as I eternally retreat.